KEY VOCABULARY FOR WORLD HISTORY

John Marshall Carter

ISBN: 978-1-304-99698-5

CONTENTS

Key Vocabulary for River Valley Civilizations

1. Civilization
2. Irrigation
3. Artisans
4. Division of labor
5. Artifacts
6. Culture
7. Lucy
8. Agriculture
9. Domestication
10. Homo sapiens
11. Neanderthals
12. Cro-Magnon
13. Hominids
14. Paleolithic Age
15. Neolithic Age
16. Hieroglyphics
17. Papyrus
18. Dynasty
19. Monotheism
20. Polytheism
21. Herodotus

22. Menes
23. Hyksos
24. Pharaoh
25. Empire
26. Thutmose III
27. Hatshepsut
28. Rameses II
29. Scribes
30. Mummification
31. Fertile Crescent
32. Mesopotamia
33. Cuneiform
34. City-state
35. Howard Carter
36. Sumer
37. Ur
38. Sumerians
39. Sargon I
40. Akkadians
41. Babylonians
42. Hammurabi
43. Code of Hammurabi
44. Hittites
45. Assyrians

World History Ancient India and China

1. Indus River
2. Ganges River
3. Monsoons
4. Citadel
5. Mohenjo-Daro
6. Harappa
7. Indo-Aryans
8. Vedas
9. Sanskrit
10. Vedic Age
11. Dravidians
12. Brahmins
13. Raja
14. Hinduism
15. Buddhism
16. Upanishads
17. Ramayana
18. Bhagavad Gita
19. Varnas
20. Caste system
21. Monism
22. maya
23. Brahman
24. Atman
25. Reincarnation
26. Nirvana
27. Brahma
28. Vishnu
29. Siva
30. Siddhartha Gautama
31. Buddha
32. Four Noble Truths
33. The Eightfold Path
34. Theravada Buddhism
35. Mahayana Buddhism

36. Huang He
37. Yangtze
38. Loess
39. Xia
40. Shang
41. Zhou
42. Era of Warring States
43. Qin
44. Han
45. "Mandate of Heaven"
46. Confucius
47. Lao-tzu
48. Confucianism
49. Daoism
50. Legalism
51. Shi Huangdi
52. Liu Bang
53. Great Wall of China

Key Vocabulary for Ancient China

1. Huang He
2. Yangtze
3. Yellow River
4. Dikes
5. Xia Dynasty
6. Shang Dynasty
7. Kaolin
8. Oracle bones
9. Zhou Dynasty
10. Qin Dynasty
11. Han Dynasty
12. Great Wall of China
13. Civil service exam
14. Leveling
15. Silk Road
16. Ying
17. Yang
18. Analects
19. Laozi
20. Confucius
21. Dao De Jing
22. Legalism
23. Buddhism
24. Genealogy
25. Five Classics
26. The Book of History
27. The Book of Poems
28. The Book of Changes
29. The Book of Rites
30. Acupuncture
31. Xiongnu

Key Vocabulary for Ancient Greece

1. Minoans
2. Mycenaeans
3. Crete
4. Knossos
5. Frescoes
6. Aegean Sea
7. Polis
8. City-state
9. Acropolis
10. Agora
11. The Iliad
12. The Odyssey
13. Homer
14. Myths
15. Olympic Games
16. Aristocracy
17. Plutocracy
18. Democracy
19. Monarchy
20. Phalanx
21. Hoplites
22. Tyrant
23. Sparta
24. Athens
25. Corinth
26. Thebes
27. Helots
28. Areopagus
29. Ephors
30. Gerousia
31. Archon
32. Metics
33. Draco
34. Solon
35. Cleisthenes
36. Assembly of 500
37. Pisistratus

38. Direct democracy
39. Sappho
40. Sophists
41. Rhetoric
42. Plato
43. Aristotle
44. Socrates
45. Ethics
46. Philosophy
47. Persian Wars
48. Herodotus
49. Cyrus
50. Darius I
51. Xerxes
52. Battle of Marathon
53. Battle of Thermopylae
54. Battle of Plataea
55. Battle of Salamis
56. Themistocles
57. Delian League
58. Pericles
59. The Peloponnesian War
60. Thucydides

KEY VOCABULARY ANCIENT ROME

1. Romulus
2. Republic
3. Consul
4. Senate
5. Dictator
6. Veto
7. Praetors
8. Tribunes
9. Patricians
10. Plebeians
11. Conflict of the Orders
12. Legion
13. Carthage
14. Punic Wars
15. Hannibal
16. Battle of Cannae
17. Scipio
18. Battle of Zama
19. Spartacus
20. Equites
21. The Gracchi
22. Gaius Marius
23. Lucius Sulla
24. First Triumvirate
25. Julius Caesar
26. Gnaeus Pompey
27. Licinius Crassus
28. Cleopatra
29. Second Triumvirate
30. Octavian
31. Mark Antony
32. Augustus
33. Pax Romana
34. Julio-Claudian Emperors
35. Five Good Emperors
36. Hadrian
37. Gladiators

38. Ptolemy (Claudius)
39. Virgil
40. Tacitus
41. Plutarch
42. Ovid
43. Aqueducts
44. Rabbis
45. Jesus of Nazareth
46. Gospels
47. Messiah
48. Martyrs
49. Bishops
50. Patriarchs
51. Pope
52. Council of Nicaea
53. The Trinity
54. Marcus Aurelius
55. Inflation
56. Diocletian
57. Constantine
58. Visigoths
59. Ostrogoths
60. Vandals

KEY VOCABULARY FOR EARLY AFRICA

1. Mohammed I Askia
2. Songhai
3. Mansa Musa
4. Tunka Manin
5. Timbuktu
6. Ghana
7. Mali
8. Al-Bakri
9. Great Zimbabwe
10. Shona
11. Swahili
12. Mombasa
13. Kilwa
14. Mogadishu
15. King Ezana
16. Aksum
17. Dhow
18. Meroe
19. Kush
20. Nubia
21. Matrilineal
22. Linguists
23. Bantu
24. Oral traditions
25. Plateau
26. Savannas
27. Tropical rain forest
28. Kalahari
29. Namib
30. Kilimanjaro

KEY VOCABULARY : THE AMERICAS

1. Potlatches
2. Hohokam
3. Anasazi
4. Bering Strait
5. Quechua
6. Quipu
7. Inca
8. Toltecs
9. Chichen Itza
10. Chinampas
11. Aztecs
12. Technotitlan
13. Texcoco
14. Cuzco
15. Juanita
16. Mayans
17. Olmecs
18. Chavin
19. Andes
20. MesoAmerica
21. Hopewell
22. Mississippians
23. Adobe
24. Tepees
25. Pueblo

KEY VOCABULARY : THE AMERICAS

1. Potlatches
2. Hohokam
3. Anasazi
4. Bering Strait
5. Quechua
6. Quipu
7. Inca
8. Toltecs
9. Chichen Itza
10. Chinampas
11. Aztecs
12. Technotitlan
13. Texcoco
14. Cuzco
15. Juanita
16. Mayans
17. Olmecs
18. Chavin
19. Andes
20. MesoAmerica
21. Hopewell
22. Mississippians
23. Adobe
24. Tepees
25. Pueblo

KEY VOCABULARY FOR THE Islamic World (ca. 570 to 1250 A.D.)

1. Muhammad
2. Khadija
3. Ali
4. Kaaba
5. Muslims
6. Mecca
7. Medina
8. Hijrah
9. Islam
10. Qu'ran
11. Caliph
12. Umar
13. Mosques
14. Jihad
15. Abu Bakr
16. Sunni
17. Shiah (Shi'ites)
18. Imams
19. Sufi
20. Moors
21. Tariq
22. Sultan
23. Al-Razi
24. Ibn Sina
25. Al-Idrisi
26. Astrolabe
27. Minaret
28. "The Thousand and One Nights"
29. Bedouins
30. Quraysh
31. Zamzam
32. Umma
33. Five Pillars of Islam
34. Umayyad Caliphate
35. Jizra
36. Abassid Caliphate
37. Harun al-Rashid

38. Ulama
39. Shari'a
40. Sufis
41. Mamluks

Key Vocabulary for Inner and East Asia

1. Sui
2. Grand Canal
3. Tang
4. Li Bo
5. Du Fu
6. Empress Wu
7. Zen
8. Zhao Kuangyin
9. Civil service exam
10. Diamond Sutra
11. Temujin
12. Karakorum
13. Genghis Khan
14. Kublai Khan
15. Batu
16. Golden Horde
17. Marco Polo
18. "The Travels of Marco Polo"
19. Shintoism
20. Kami
21. "The Tale of Genji"
22. Fujiwara
23. Minamoto
24. Shogun
25. Ashikaga
26. Bushido
27. Samurai
28. Daimyo
29. Zen Buddhism
30. Silla
31. Koryo
32. Sejong
33. Annam

34. Khmer Empire
35. catapults
36. Yurts
37. Mongols
38. Shamanism

KEY VOCABULARY FOR EUROPE IN THE MIDDLE AGES

1. Medieval
2. Clovis
3. Merovingians
4. Charles Martel
5. Carolingians
6. Charlemagne
7. Missi dominici
8. Alcuin
9. Louis the Pious
10. Magyars
11. Vikings
12. Feudalism
13. Fief
14. Vassal
15. Primogeniture
16. Stirrup
17. Manorialism
18. Serfs
19. Chivalry
20. Pope
21. Bishop
22. Parish priest
23. Cardinals
24. Curia
25. Saint Benedict
26. Abbot
27. Abbess
28. Canon law
29. Heretics
30. Simony
31. Inquisition
32. Anglo-Saxons
33. Alfred the Great
34. Edward the Confessor
35. William the Conqueror
36. The Bayeux Tapestry
37. Domesday Book

38. Henry II
39. Thomas Becket
40. Eleanor of Aquitaine
41. King John
42. Magna Carta
43. Parliament
44. The Capetians
45. Otto I
46. Henry IV
47. Pope Gregory VII
48. Frederick Barbarossa
49. Innocent III
50. Bubonic Plague

KEY VOCABULARY FOR THE RENAISSANCE AND REFORMATION

1. Renaissance
2. Michelangelo
3. Da Vinci
4. Baldasare Castiglione
5. Niccolo Machiaelli
6. Humanists
7. Shakespeare
8. Erasmus
9. Pieter Brueghel the Elder
10. Albrecht Duerer
11. Hans Holbein
12. Jan van Eyck
13. Reformation
14. Protestants
15. Catholics
16. Indulgences
17. Martin Luther
18. John Calvin
19. Ulrich Zwingli
20. "95 Theses"
21. *Institutes of the Christian Religion*
22. Sects

23.Counter Reformation

24.Inquisition

25. Pope Paul III

26.Pope Leo X

27.Council of Worms

28.Emperor Charles V

29.Henry VIII of England

30.Charles I of England

31.Oliver Cromwell

32. English Civil War

33.Elizabeth I of England

34.Phillip II of Spain

35.Thirty Years War

36.Henry IV of France

37.Edict of Nantes

38.Huguenots

39.Puritans

40.Interregnum

41. Council of Trent

Key Vocabulary for The Age of Exploration and Discovery

1. Tariffs
2. Joint-stock company
3. Heliocentric theory
4. Middle Passage
5. Hernan Cortes
6. Francisco Pizarro
7. King Phillip II
8. Christopher Columbus
9. Vasco da Gama
10. Bartholomew Diaz
11. Galileo Galilei
12. Mercantilism
13. Nicolaus Copernicus
14. Roger Bacon
15. Scientific Revolution
16. Geocentric theory
17. Johannes Kepler
18. Isaac Newton
19. Andreas Vesalius
20. William Harvey
21. Francis Bacon
22. Renes Descartes
23. Robert Boyle
24. Commercial Revolution
25. Compass
26. Astrolabe
27. Favorable balance of trade
28. Prince Henry the Navigator
29. Marco Polo
30. Queen Isabella
31. Treaty of Tordesillas
32. Ferdinand Magellan
33. Amerigo Vespucci
34. Triangular trade
35. Ponce de Leon
36. Moctezuma II
37. Emperor Charles V

38. William of Orange
39. Guerrilla warfare
40. Pedro Cabral

Key Vocabulary for Asia in Transition

1. Ming Dynasty
2. Junks
3. Hsuan-yeh
4. Qing Dynasty
5. Nurhachi
6. Manchus
7. Zhu Yuanzhang (Hung Wu)
8. Queue
9. Philology
10. White Lotus Rebellion
11. Opium War
12. Treaty of Nanjing
13. “unequal” treaties
14. The Taiping Rebelling
15. Tokugawa Shogunate
16. Oda Nobunaga
17. Toyotomi Hideyoshi
18. Tokugawa Ieyasu
19. Edo
20. Daimyos
21. Samurai
22. Kabuki theater
23. Matthew Perry

24. Treaty of Kanagawa

25. consulates

KEY VOCABULARY FOR ISLAMIC

EMPIRES IN ASIA

1. Delhi Sultanate
2. Tamerlane
3. Ottomans
4. Ghazis
5. Kizilbash
6. Esmail
7. Abbas
8. Jahangir
9. Shah Jahan
10. Janissaries
11. Millets
12. Babur
13. Suleyman the Magnificent
14. Istanbul
15. Isfahan (or, Esfahan)
16. Delhi
17. Aurangzeb
18. Jizra
19. Sunni
20. Shi'ites
21. Nanak
22. Sikh

23. Akbar

24. Rajputs

25. Tahmasp

26. Shah

27. Safi-od-Din

28. Reaya

29. Mehmed II

30. Timur

31. Battle of Chaldiran

32. Battle of Ankara

KEY VOCABULARY FOR THE AGE OF ABSOLUTISM

1. Louis XIV
2. St. Petersburg
3. Burgesses
4. Parliament
5. Queen Elisabeth I
6. Mary Queen of Scots
7. Puritans
8. Spanish Armada
9. Seven Years' War
10. Frederick the Great
11. Diplomatic Revolution
12. Frederick William I
13. Maria Theresa
14. Pragmatic Sanction
15. The Partitions of Poland
16. Peter the Great
17. Michael Romanov
18. Czar
19. Balance of power
20. War of the Spanish Succession
21. Jean-Baptiste Colbert
22. Divine Right of Kings
23. "L'etat c'est moi"
24. Versailles
25. The Sun King
26. The Thirty Years' War
27. Cardinal Richelieu
28. intendants

Key Vocabulary for the Scientific Revolution and the Enlightenment

1. Roger Bacon
2. Scientific Revolution
3. Claudius Ptolemy
4. Nicolaus Copernicus
5. Geocentric
6. Heliocentric
7. Galileo Galilei
8. Johannes Kepler
9. Tycho Brahe
10. Isaac Newton
11. Andreas Vesalius
12. William Harvey
13. Rene' Descartes
14. Francis Bacon
15. Robert Boyle
16. Joseph Priestly
17. Antoine Lavoisier
18. Philosophes
19. The Encyclopedia
20. Rationalism
21. Denis Diderot
22. Baron de Montesquieu
23. Voltaire
24. John Locke
25. Thomas Hobbes
26. Mary Wallstonecraft
27. Age of Enlightenment

KEY VOCABULARY FOR THE AMERICAN REVOLUTION

1. French and Indian War
2. Stamp Act
3. King George III
4. Lord North
5. Patriots
6. Loyalists
7. "no taxation without representation"
8. British East India Company
9. Boston Tea Party
10. Declaration of Independence
11. Thomas Jefferson
12. Mercenaries
13. George Washington
14. Battle of Saratoga
15. John Burgoyne
16. Benjamin Franklin
17. Battle of Yorktown
18. Articles of Confederation
19. Federal system of government
20. Executive Branch
21. Legislative Branch
22. Judicial Branch
23. Bill of Rights

KEY VOCABULARY FOR THE FRENCH REVOLUTION AND NAPOLEON

1. Republic
2. Declaration of the Rights of Man
3. Marquis de Lafayette
4. Estates General
5. Bourgeoisie
6. National Assembly
7. Louis XVI
8. The Bastille
9. The Great Fear
10. Maximilien Robespierre
11. Edmund Burke
12. Mary Wollstonecraft
13. Marie Antoinette
14. Jacobins
15. Guillotine
16. National Convention
17. Girondists
18. The Mountain
19. Georges Danton
20. Battle of Valmy
21. Reign of Terror
22. Sans-culottes
23. Committee of Public Safety
24. The Directory
25. Napoleon Bonaparte
26. Civil Code of 1804
27. Concordat of 1801
28. Battle of Austerlitz
29. Treaty of Tilsit
30. Battle of Trafalgar
31. Battle of Borodino
32. Klemens von Metternich
33. Quadruple Alliance
34. Elba
35. Louis XVIII
36. Battle of Waterloo
37. Congress of Vienna

KEY VOCABULARY FOR THE INDUSTRIAL REVOLUTION

1. Industrial Revolution
2. Jethro Tull
3. Enclosure movement
4. Crop rotation
5. Factors of production
6. Capital
7. Mechanization
8. Factory system
9. Richard Arkwright
10. Eli Whitney
11. Thomas Newcomen
12. James Watt
13. Henry Bessemer
14. Vulcanization
15. George Stephenson
16. Robert Fulton
17. Samuel Morse
18. Wage system
19. Elizabeth Bently
20. Tenements
21. Capitalism
22. Division of labor
23. Interchangeable parts
24. Mass production
25. Henry Ford
26. Corporations
27. J.P. Morgan
28. Monopoly
29. Cartels
30. Business cycle
31. Depression
32. Adam Smith
33. Free enterprise

34. Thomas Malthus
35. David Ricardo
36. Laissez-faire
37. Humanitarians
38. Charles Dickens
39. Jeremy Bentham
40. Utilitarianism
41. John Stuart Mill
42. Strike
43. Unions
44. Means of production
45. Utopian socialists
46. Robert Owen
47. Karl Marx
48. Friedrich Engels
49. Bourgeoisie
50. Proletariat
51. Communism
52. Democratic socialism

Key Vocabulary For The Age of Nationalism

1. Risorgimento
2. Carbonari
3. Giuseppe Mazzini
4. Young Italy Movement
5. King Victor Emmanuel II
6. Camill Benso di Cavour
7. Napoleon III
8. Giuseppe Garibaldi
9. Junkers
10. Wars of Unification
11. Treaty of Prague
12. Otto von Bismarck
13. Kaiser
14. Bundesrat
15. Reichstag
16. Kulturkampf
17. Social Democratic Party
18. William II
19. Autocrat
20. Russification
21. Alexander II
22. Emancipation Edict
23. People's Will
24. Terrorism
25. Pogroms
26. Duma
27. Francis Joseph I
28. Treaty of San Stefano
29. Balkan League

KEY VOCABULARY FOR THE AGE OF IMPERIALISM

1. Imperialism
2. Settlement colonies
3. Spheres of influence
4. "The White Man's Burden"
5. Rudyard Kipling
6. Missionaries
7. Sultan Moulay Abd al-Hafid
8. Suez Canal
9. Al-Mahdi
10. Fashoda crisis
11. Samory Toure
12. Henry Stanley
13. King Leopold II
14. Shaka Zulu
15. Afrikaans
16. Boers
17. Cecil Rhodes
18. Boer War
19. Paternalism
20. Menelik II
21. Assimilation
22. Meiji Restoration
23. Diet
24. Sino-Japanese
25. Treaty of Shimonoseki
26. King Mongkut
27. Queen Liliuokalani
28. Emilio Aguinaldo
29. The Maine
30. The Treaty of Paris
31. Theodore Roosevelt
32. Panama Canal
33. Roosevelt Corollary
34. Carlos Juan Finlay
35. Victoriano Huerta
36. Emiliano Zapata
37. Pancho Villa

Key Vocabulary For World War I

1. Nationalism
2. Imperialism
3. Militarism
4. Alliances
5. Mobilize
6. Dreadnought
7. Triple Alliance
8. Triple Entente
9. Balkan “powder keg”
10. Archduke Franz Ferdinand
11. Ultimatum
12. Belligerents
13. Central Powers
14. U-boats
15. Propaganda
16. Gallipoli
17. Woodrow Wilson
18. War of attrition
19. Contraband
20. Arthur Zimmermann
21. Russian Revolution
22. Vladimir Lenin
23. Bolsheviks
24. Duma
25. Mensheviks
26. Red Army
27. Fourteen Points
28. Treaty of Versailles
29. Armistice
30. Reparations
31. League of Nations
32. Genocide
33. World Court
34. Economic sanctions

Key Vocabulary For The Interwar Years

1. Influenza pandemic
2. Oswald Spengler
3. Gertrude Stein
4. Franz Kafka
5. Surrealism
6. James Joyce
7. T.S. Eliot
8. Igor Stravinsky
9. Pablo Picasso
10. Salvador Dali
11. Dadaists
12. Louis Sullivan
13. Functionalism
14. Frank Lloyd Wright
15. Prohibition
16. "flappers"
17. Economic nationalism
18. Market speculations
19. Black Tuesday
20. Great Depression
21. Herbert Hoover
22. Franklin D. Roosevelt
23. New Deal
24. Social Security Act
25. Maginot Line
26. Locarno Pact
27. General strike
28. Popular Front
29. Leon Blum
30. Nationalization
31. Ramsay McDonald
32. Easter Rising
33. Sinn Fein
34. Benito Mussolini
35. Fascism

36. Black Shirts
37. Corporatist state
38. Adolf Hitler
39. Nazi Party
40. Reichstag
41. Third Reich
42. Rome-Berlin Axis
43. Collective farms
44. Leon Trotsky
45. Vladimir Lenin
46. Josef Stalin
47. Command economy
48. Five-year Plan
49. Purge
50. Comintern

Key Vocabulary For World Nationalist Movements

1. Wafd Party
2. Anglo-Egyptian Treaty
3. Zionism
4. Mohandas Gandhi
5. Mustafa Kemal
6. Reza Shah Pahlavi
7. Nnamdi Azikiwe
8. Jomo Kenyatta
9. Leopold Senghor
10. Open Door Policy
11. Boxer Rebellion
12. Empress Dowager Tz'u-his
13. Kuomintang
14. Sun Yixian
15. Chiang Kai-shek
16. Long March
17. Mao Zedong
18. Russo-Japanese War
19. The Treaty of Portsmouth
20. Rafael Trujillo Molina
21. Anastasio Somoza
22. Fulgencio Batista
23. Lazaro Cardenas

Key Vocabulary For World War II

1. Kellogg-Briand Pact
2. Osachi Hamaguchi
3. Spanish Civil War
4. Francisco Franco Falange
5. International Brigades
6. Anti-Comintern Pact
7. Axis Powers
8. Munich Conference
9. Neville Chamberlain
10. Edouard Daladier
11. German-Soviet Non-Aggression Pact
12. Blitzkrieg
13. Collaborators
14. "phony war"
15. Philippe Petain
16. Charles de Gaulle
17. Maquis
18. Battle of Britain
19. Neutrality Acts
20. Isolationists
21. Lend-Lease Act
22. Atlantic Charter
23. Winston Churchill
24. Erwin Rommel
25. Final Solution
26. Holocaust
27. Heinrich Himmler
28. Wannsee Conference
29. Auschwitz
30. Anne Frank
31. Battle of Stalingrad
32. Dwight D. Eisenhower
33. "soft underbelly of the Axis"
34. Battle of Midway
35. Operation Overlord

36. D-Day
37. V-E Day
38. Yalta Conference
39. Bataan Death March

Key Vocabulary For Asia Since 1945

1.Muslim League

2.Muhammad Ali Jinnah

3. Jawaharlal Nehru

4. Indira Nehru Gandhi

5. mixed economy

6.Dalai Lama

7. Awami League

8. Benazir Bhutto

9. Mao Zedong

10. Great Leap Forward

11. Cultural Revolution

12. Deng Xiaoping

13. Tiananmen Square Massacre

14. Kim Il Sung

15. Syngman Rhee

16. SCAP

17."MacArthur Constitution"

18. zaibatsu

19. Liberal-Democratic Party

20. Ferdinand Marcos

21. Corazon Aquino

22. Aung Suu Kyi

23. Ho Chi Minh

24. Battle of Dien Bien Phu

25. domino theory

26. Tet Offensive

27. Paris Peace Accords

28. Khmer Rouge

29. Pol Pot

30. ASEAN

31. “Four Tigers”

Key Vocabulary for Africa and the Middle East Since 1945

1. Kwame Nkrumah
2. Pan-Africanism
3. Mau Mau
4. Jomo Kenyata
5. Apartheid
6. Nelson Mandela
7. Desmond Tutu
8. Steven Biko
9. F.W. de Klerk
10. Tutsi
11. Hutu
12. Laurent Kabila
13. Desertification
14. Shaaban Robert
15. Colons
16. Menachem Begin
17. Abdel Nasser
18. Kibbutz
19. Suez Crisis
20. Abd al-Aziz Ibn Sa'ud
21. Mohammad Mosaddeq
22. Shah Mohammad Reza Pahlavi
23. Mustafa Kemal
24. Ismet Inonu
25. Six-Day War
26. PLO
27. Yasir Arafat
28. Golda Meir
29. Anwar Sadat
30. Camp David Accords
31. Intifada
32. OPEC
33. Iranian Revolution
34. Ayatollah Khomeini
35. Yom Kippur War
36. Saddam Hussein
37. Kurds

38. Operation Desert Shield
39. Operation Desert Storm

Key Vocabulary For Latin America Since 1945

1. Multinational corporations
2. Monoculture
3. Import substitution
4. NAFTA
5. Mothers of the Plaza de Mayo
6. Organization of American States
7. PRI
8. Carlos Salinas de Gortari
9. Vicente Fox
10. Daniel Ortega
11. Contras
12. Violeta Barrios de Chamorro
13. FMLN
14. Contadora Principles
15. Oscar Arias
16. Fidel Castro
17. Ernesto "Che " Guevara
18. Bay of Pigs Invasion
19. Dissidents
20. Luis Munoz
21. Operation Bootstrap
22. Jean-Claude Duvalier
23. Jean-Bertrand Aristide
24. Juan Peron
25. Desaparecidos
26. The Falklands
27. Shining Path
28. Salvador Allende

Key Vocabulary For The West in the Post-War World

1. United Nations
2. Nurnberg Trials
3. Eleanor Roosevelt
4. General Assembley
5. United Nations
6. Security Council
7. The Cold War
8. The Truman Doctrine
9. Containment
10. Marshall Plan
11. Berlin Airlift
12. Warsaw Pact
13. NATO
14. Welfare state
15. Common Market
16. European Community
17. Nikita Khrushchev
18. Joseph McCarthy
19. John F. Kennedy
20. Lyndon Johnson
21. Richard Nixon
22. NAACP
23. Martin Luther King, Jr.
24. Southeast Asia Treaty Organization
25. Cuban missile crisis
26. DEW Line

Key Vocabulary For Superpowers in the Modern Era

1. Richard Nixon
2. Vietnamization
3. Paris Peace Accords
4. Watergate
5. Jimmy Carter
6. Ronald Reagan
7. Iran-contra affair
8. Bill Clinton
9. George W. Bush
10. Détente
11. Carter Doctrine
12. Weapons of Mass Destruction
13. Pierre Trudeau
14. NAFTA
15. Margaret Thatcher
16. Tony Blair
17. Irish Republican Army
18. Georges Pompidou
19. Francois Mitterand
20. Willy Brandt
21. Ostpolitik
22. Helmut Kohl
23. Juan Carlos
24. Andreas Papandreu
25. Helsinki Accords
26. NATO
27. European Union
28. Maastricht Treaty
29. Leonid Brezhnev
30. Brezhnev Doctrine
31. Mikhail Gorbachev
32. Perestroika
33. Glasnost
34. Boris Yeltsin
35. Commonwealth of Independent States
36. Vaclav Havel
37. Lech Walesa

38. Slobadan Milosevic
39. Ethnic cleansing
40. World Trade Center
41. Pentagon
42. 9/11/2001
43. Rudolph Giuliani
44. al Qaeda
45. Osama bin Laden
46. Tom Ridge
47. Office of Homeland Security
48. Colin Powell
49. Taliban

www.ingramcontent.com/pod-product-compliance
Ingram Content Group UK Ltd.
Pitfield, Milton Keynes, MK11 3LW, UK
UKHW041835200726
13854UKWH00003BA/1151

9 781304 996985